101

TIPS FOR
KINDERGARTEN
AT HOME

101

TIPS FOR KINDERGARTEN AT HOME

Start Homeschooling with Confidence

ADRIANA ZODER

Book Layout and Cover Design by: Emily Davidson

ALSO by ADRIANA ZODER

101 Tips for Preschool at Home

To my children, who teach me every day

Please visit Adriana Zoder's blog, www.HomeschoolWays.com, to claim a FREE book, 21 Days to Jumpstart Your Homeschool. Written for homeschooling parents who need to (re)start their homeschool experience, this ebook will uncover simple solutions for guaranteed results. Part devotional and part workbook, this step-by-step guide helps you achieve more and stress less.

ACKNOWLEDGMENTS

This book would not have been possible without the gentle guidance of the Holy Spirit, the support of my husband, and the patience of my children.

CONTENTS

INTRODUCTION

Please know that I wrote this book to help homeschooling parents, not to challenge them. The education of our children is not a race in any form. It is a journey to be enjoyed and made as pleasant as possible, for all parties involved.

In his seminal TED talk on education, *How Schools Kill Creativity*, Sir Ken Robinson laughed at people who said that kindergarten was college. He set the record straight: "Kindergarten is kindergarten." I agree.

Let your child enjoy his kindergarten year. Make sure you enjoy your child's kindergarten year. Don't over schedule activities outside the home and don't overbuy curriculum.

Jean Piaget, the Swiss psychologist famous for his theories on the stages of children's development, while lecturing in the US in the 1960s, kept getting what he called the American Question: "How can we speed these stages up?" His comeback was, "Why would you want to do that?"[1]

Don't rush. Haste makes waste. In the words of Ann Voskamp, "Slow. Children at play. Hurry hurts kids."[2]

Plan some field trips, time spent in nature, and not so much seat work. Plan for unscheduled play time. Read to your child and turn off the TV. Turn off any other electronic devices while you're at it.

Go low-tech. Your child will sit in front of computers throughout his adult life anyway. Let him enjoy his childhood away from screens. He won't miss a thing. On the contrary, it will help him figure the world in a concrete, 3D way.

As you read this book, like with anything else, choose those activities that fit your homeschool. This book is organized in ten chapters, each with ten tips. The eleventh chapter contains tip number 101.

101 Tips for Kindergarten at Home is the second volume in my *How to Homeschool* series. The first volume, *101 Tips for Preschool at Home*, follows the same easy-to-read format and provides a great foundation for your homeschool journey, including homeschool methodologies, field trip tips, essential reference titles for homeschool educators and more.

I started writing this series because I read way too many long books on homeschooling. My children were in diapers, I was sleep deprived, and my values on education were not entirely clear. I was poking at homeschooling from all angles to see if it was my tired mind playing tricks on me or if God was truly calling my name.

I wished for a simple book that explained in quick, easy-to-follow steps how to prepare for homeschooling, what pitfalls to avoid, and how to achieve success while keeping stress to a minimum. As I gained more knowledge and went through a series of providential events, God's call for me to homeschool my children was unmistakable. But... I was not interested. I felt unworthy, unprepared, and oh, so tired.

Frankly, I also felt unwilling to put my career plans to the sidelines for the next 15 years or so. Wasn't it enough that I stayed home with my children for the first five years of their lives?

As I continued to pray and study, I remembered He Who calls is faithful. He qualifies the called. He will guide me. The ride will be a blessed one because of His presence. So far, He has not disappointed.

As to a career outside the home, God has given me peace and the understanding that homeschooling and homemaking are careers.

Finally, a few technicalities... You can read the chapters in the order that interests you.

Please note that I am referring to a child as a "he" in this book. I hope you will not be offended. I realize many of you have daughters in kindergarten.

In most languages I know, "child" is a masculine noun. Also, I think it is awkward to write "he/she" or "his/her" or "him/her" throughout the book. Last but not least, writing about a child and then referring to "their" education seems grammatically wrong to me.

Thank you for reading!

CHAPTER 1:

10 REASONS TO EMBRACE

KINDERGARTEN AT HOME

*"I would walk without my shoes to the end of the Earth, I would give up
anything I had to, to teach you self-worth." – Jayne Sena
"What I Would Do For You" (a mother to child poem)*

Today, people homeschool for so many reasons. Secular
people with cool jobs board planes to fly all over the world while
their children come along, wheeling their designer school bags
around airports. Religious people like the idea of keeping their
children away from worldly influences, so they homeschool them.

Parents of children with learning differences prefer to give
them one-on-one attention at home and, thus, avoid labels and
special education classes. Yet another category of people includes
those who believe the public school system paradigm is intrinsically
wrong socially and academically, based on research. They believe

tutoring their children at home produces better results, so they homeschool. No matter which category you fall into, you should be able to state clearly why you homeschool. To help you get started on your list, here are 10 main reasons to embrace kindergarten at home:

1. Mom is cool.

When a child is five, he still wants to be around his mom. He needs the nurturing and care and love and attention only his mom can give him. A child who is full of mom's presence through homeschooling grows up with more self-worth and a more secure self-image than children who spend 35 hours a week in a school setting. That's just my observation of my homeschooled friends versus my friends who were schooled in a traditional classroom.

A blogger shared that, during a hike, her 16-year-old was climbing a small peak with another friend, while their families were watching. As he got to the top, the blogger's son, still with his back to the family, asked his friend, "Is mom watching?" He wanted to know if his greatest fan was there, admiring his feat.

Even at 16, our children need the reassurance that mom is there, watching, being proud of their achievements. How much more at five going on six?

2. A full-day kindergarten makes for an exhausted child.

Some schools offer a half-day kindergarten. Most don't. When our oldest had to go to kindergarten, our local school had just introduced the full-day kindergarten. All the more reasons to keep him home.

A friend of mine who chooses to stay home, but puts her children in public school, told me her kindergarten-age children took a nap every day. They were that tired.

After seven hours in school, any child is exhausted, cranky, sleepy and hungry. That's who comes home. That's what you get as a parent, at the end of a school day. Why should others enjoy your child while he is rested? Why should you get shortchanged like that?

3. It's a jungle out there.

Socialization does not happen at school. Survival happens at school. Children learn how to negotiate peer-pressure on their own and it's not a pretty picture.

The local doctors and lawyers may be sending their children to your neighborhood school, but so do drug addicts and welfare queens. Your kindergartner is too young to discern who is a good companion and who is not. And, sometimes, we must avoid both the preacher's kids and the posh kids.

I am sure you can think of wonderful children you went to school with, who came from bad neighborhoods, and vice versa. Discernment and the ability to choose friends wisely comes later, not when one is five going on six.

4. School is very different from when you and I attended.

This working mom told me her daughter, who was in kindergarten, told her, "Mommy, Carl said that he wanted to make sexy with Mary. What does that mean?" Stunned, the mom asked her if the daughter asked Carl what he meant. She said, "Yes, I did. Carl said that when a girl gets on top of a boy and they kiss, they make sexy." Sighing, this mom wished she did not have to work. "I thought of you when this happened," she said. "I really wish I could homeschool my children."

Well, finances and homeschooling are a different subject altogether, but the point is, if you want to shelter your children from a society that has gone sex-crazy, homeschooling is the way to go.

5. You have the freedom to switch curriculum.

During my son's kindergarten year, we switched math curriculum mid-semester. Just like that. Six weeks into Singapore Math, it became clear that he was bored and needed a different program, something more challenging and maybe not so traditional. After looking around, I discovered Right Start Mathematics. Their online placement test put my son on Level B, which roughly corresponds to first grade. Their Montessori approach worked better for my active boy and their fast pace kept him challenged, i.e. not bored out of his mind. After we switched, he asked to do math even before breakfast. How cool is that!

6. You have the freedom to have no curriculum at all.

Kindergarten is all about introducing your child to the experience of learning. You can do kindergarten for free. Just go to your local library and let your child pick books he likes. Then, read them to him. If he seems interested in a certain topic, go back to the library the next day and get some more books on that particular subject. Take a field trip to a place that teaches even more about it.

Rinse. Repeat. It can be that easy.

Now, if you want a more systematic approach to your child's reading matter, you can Google "reading lists for kindergarten students" and take your pick. Or invest in *Books Children Love* by Elizabeth Wilson and *The Well-Trained Mind* by Susan Wise Bower – they have lists of books organized by topics and/or school grades. You cannot go wrong.

7. You want to stay home with your younger children.

Why struggle to put a baby and/or a toddler in the car at 7:30am, to drive your five-year-old to school for kindergarten? Why interrupt the afternoon naps to go get your oldest from school? Many moms of preschoolers find it easier to homeschool the kindergartner while staying home with all their children. At least once a week, consider spending time with other homeschooling moms and their children – outside. Enjoy the adult conversation as your children play together. You will not feel as isolated.

Bring a sack lunch, water, and a few books. The children will occupy themselves, the baby will nap or nurse happily, and life will be a lot smoother. Plus the memories and the bonds you establish will last a lifetime.

8. You don't have to be away from your child for 35+ hours a week.

I can't imagine being away from my children for that long, can you? I would miss them so.

As I was deciding to homeschool, I simply could not wrap my mind around the enormous amount of time children must spend away from their parents in the name of education.

Love is spelled T-I-M-E. Have you ever watched Franklin – the cartoon? It's a great cartoon with lots of life lessons and no violence. The kids are respectful to adults and the adults act responsibly. I'm not advocating for your children to watch cartoons. But if they do, an episode of Franklin would be much better than anything else out there. Having said all that, have you ever listened – really listened – to the words of the Franklin song? "Hey, it's Franklin... with all his friends... they got stories ... got time to spend... with you..."

Time. Franklin has time for your children. Do you?

9. You have control over your children's influences.

Peer pressure to make immature decisions, based on anything but biblical principles, is at an all time high. Social media and technology have taken good old peer pressure to new heights. These days, teenagers commit suicide because of something somebody said on social media about them.

This prison staff member shared that in his facility they took a survey of the inmates. When asked "What is the one thing that got you into prison?" the majority of inmates answered, "My friends." They all wished their parents had monitored their choice of friends better.[3] This peer-dependence does not come upon them over night. It has been cultivated since kindergarten. After all, school children spend more time with each other than with their parents.

Our children need the safety of the family home to develop discernment and establish good habits. They can go witness to the world once they are equipped. A five-year-old is not equipped to withstand social pressures inviting him to go against his family's lifestyle.

A homeschooling mom of four told me, "I can overhear all the conversations my children are having throughout the day." If she put her children in a school for 35+ hours a week, she could not say the same thing.

10. A solid education does not take seven hours a day.

If you grew up in a country where school is seven hours a day, you might have a hard time coming out of that paradigm. But think about it for a moment. Did Thomas Jefferson go to school for seven hours a day, 180 days of the year? How about Michelangelo? Or any other genius in this earth's history?

Researchers have calculated that teachers spend 7-13 minutes per day in actual instruction.[4] The rest of the time is spent in discipline, classroom management, assemblies, lunch, recess and goodness knows what else. But not imparting knowledge.

Growing up in Romania, I attended school for four hours in primary school, five hours in middle school and six hours in high school. There was no kindergarten. We entered first grade at six going on seven. And we received a rigorous education.

We did not eat lunch away from parents. We had small ten-minute breaks at the end of every 50-minute class interval. One could eat a sandwich during those breaks, sitting quietly at his desk.

Perhaps that is why I have an easier time accepting a different schedule. I see a seven-hour school day as one big babysitting service for working parents.

CHAPTER 2:

10 LESSONS FROM OUR

KINDERGARTEN YEAR

*"Good judgment comes from experience. Experience comes
from bad judgment." – Jim Horning*

Where we live, we have to enroll our children in school at five
going on six. After daddy and I got on the same page about
homeschooling, the adventure began.

Our son was five and his sister was three at the time. He was in
kindergarten at home – officially. We thought of her as our
preschooler. I only worked with her through some preschool
materials because she showed interest. Otherwise, she sat with us and
absorbed everything on her level. Or she played nearby, overhearing
things and learning by osmosis, no doubt.

The main reason we decided to homeschool our children is time. I could not wrap my mind around my children spending seven hours away from me every day in the name of education. I speak several languages and have a college degree. I figured I could manage to educate my children.

So here are 10 lessons from our first homeschooling year:

1. Mommy, relax.

Seriously. You have another 12 years to teach him everything he needs to know before he heads to college. For right now, focus on life lessons more than academics. Making the bed and helping with chores around the house are just as important as the ABCs. Obedience and respecting the parents come before counting by fives.

2. Kindergarten boy, you must do your school work before you can play.

It's that simple. Now we don't spend much time on seat work, mind you. But what must be done, must be done before privileges are enjoyed. We use the *Accountable Kids* program.

My kids have cards they must accomplish in the morning, afternoon and evening. There are tickets they earn once their cards are moved from the To Do peg to the Finished peg. These tickets can be turned in to me for 30 minutes of mommy-approved cartoons or a visit to the Aquarium, for instance. At the end of the day, if all the cards are on the Finished peg, they earn a star. Once they earn ten stars, we go out for ice cream.

3. Preschool girl, sometimes you must play by yourself while mommy works with brother.

This was by far one of the toughest lessons for all of us to learn. At three going on four, my daughter did not always know what she wanted to do. Some days she claimed she wanted to be with us, but she would start interrupting. Other days, she would play quietly on the floor a few feet from us. It was only toward the end of the school year that she finally was content to play by herself while I did skill subjects like Math and Reading with my son.

4. Pray for wisdom – all of us.

I believe in doing lots of research as I homeschool. I also believe in praying for wisdom. As I made mistakes and confessed them to my children, I also shared my need of wisdom from above. Then, the light bulb came on. We all need wisdom. Even small children should know to pray for wisdom. So, at family worship time, we always prayed for wisdom. It's the best thing we can ask from God. Everything else will take care of itself if, through wisdom, we receive eyes that we may see things the way they really are.

5. Allow God to plan our homeschool schedule.

I knew I wanted my children involved in the Adventurer Club at our church. It meant driving for two hours round trip one day a week, so we could participate in a 90-minute program. A bit much, but we got settled into that routine. Besides, it was only three weeks out of the month. Because it was not exactly a weekly routine, I figured I could handle it.

Two months later, I found a violin teacher for my son who could accommodate us on that day at just the right time. Two more months later, I found a soccer program which falls on the same day and just early enough so we could commute to the violin teacher in 15 minutes.

I would have never known how to come up with such a schedule of activities one hour away from home. But God provided the right emails from my homeschool support networks, with the right information, at the right time. Also, please note that we first scheduled the most important activity – a spiritual one. Then came the activity which taught my son a skill – violin. Lastly, we added physical exercise and a team experience. We did not plan it that way, but, in retrospect, I can see God's wisdom and providence in all these details.

6. Attend craft workshops once a month.

We attend craft time for homeschoolers once a month, at the library. We tried attending twice a month, but it proved to be too much. We have a 30-minute commute to that particular library.

When we are there, the kids build something together. They don't destroy. They create. There is also a short show-and-tell program before we start the crafts. It's just an hour, but it gives everybody a chance to get to know other homeschoolers and socialize before and after the actual craft time.

I'm there with them throughout the program. I can guide them on how to behave. These are also opportunities to learn holding the door for somebody else or forgiving another child for running into them.

7. Pay attention to the stages our children are in.

This one is a corollary of the above. The previous year, I would not have made the drive (one hour both ways) to the library for craft. My daughter was still learning to potty and my son was not that keen on craft projects, as an active five-year-old boy.

But now she is four. She gives me ample warnings before I need to take her to the restroom. He, on the other hand, is showing a sudden interest in crafts and making things with his hands.

Different stages require different activities. That's what customizing our children's education looks like.

8. Spend at least two hours outside every day.

Even though we limit our children's screen time to half an hour daily, we still found that we spent too much time indoors. I wanted all of us to appreciate nature more. A camping trip with their Adventurer Club showed us how happy we all are (and how much better we sleep at night) if we spend most of the day outside.

9. Make sandwiches for lunch.

One of my stressors was finishing up school with them by 11:00am so I can start on lunch preparation. They got cranky as they got hungry, and started fighting while I was whipping up meals in the kitchen. No more. We make sandwiches for lunch. Together. Everybody is happy.

10. Don't be afraid to add a third language.

Translation: teach them French already. You see, my children are bilingual, but I have always wanted to teach them more than two languages. I have been speaking Romanian to them since birth. My husband is American, so it's all English with him. I majored in French at the University of Bucharest and, as such, I have a passion for sharing that knowledge with my children.

Toward the end of my son's kindergarten year, it finally hit me. I had to start teaching them French. I was ready.

I got all my resources lined up, including the courage to speak to them in French and add the Romanian translation right afterward.

Now, when people ask me where my children go to school, I tell them they attend a foreign language academy called "La Maison" (French for "The House").

CHAPTER 3:

10 EDUCATIONAL OBJECTIVES

FOR KINDERGARTEN

"If it is to be, it is up to me." – William H. Johnsen

Even if you take a relaxed approach to kindergarten, you should have some educational goals. Remember, you are the teacher in your homeschool. Teachers must have objectives, otherwise they will never know if they hit the target or not by the end of the year.

While you consider your objective, you will want to write things down. Over and over again, researchers have discovered that written goals get accomplished. Unwritten goals, as lovely as they may be, do not. If you do not know what your educational objectives should be, you have come to the right place. Read through this chapter and jot down what you think sounds good for your family.

Here are 10 objectives to remember as you plan your activities for the kindergarten year:

1. Introduce your kindergarten student to the process of learning.

Please note the word "introduce." Don't stress that your child does not get it, or that his craft projects are not as cute as those of another child from your homeschool group, or that he cannot read yet. The kindergarten year is about wading in the pool of learning, not swimming at its deepest points. It's not even about walking in the area where the water reaches your child's knees.

If your kindergartener spends more than one hour per school day doing worksheets, you are overdoing it. Learning can happen in so many other ways besides pen and paper.

2. Teach your child that learning is useful and, sometimes, fun.

A retired public school teacher confessed to me how nauseated she gets when she sees the emphasis on "school is fun" and educational apps which are nothing more than video games. She said that an atmosphere of enjoyment can be created while doing the hard stuff in learning – the drills and the memorization and the problem-solving. But it takes more effort on the part of the teacher. More creativity.

It also takes motivation on the part of the students. That's where the secret is. How motivated are the students? Do they know how useful it is to learn? Has anybody explained in age-appropriate ways why some people make $20,000 a year and others make $200,000 a year? And that both those people might have the same cash flow?

Tip too much on the side of usefulness and the child will get discouraged. Tip too much on the side of fun and, when it's time for hard work, the child will give up. Pray for wisdom as you seek balance. Life is not always fun and neither should be learning.

3. Show your child how to learn.

My daughter was four when she brought me a leaf and asked me what tree it was. I said I did not know. She quipped, "You can look it up on leaf.com!" She knew that, when we don't know an answer, we go online. She also knew that websites end with .com. We consult encyclopedias and reference books too, but she obviously preferred online sources.

I have not been afraid to answer "I don't know" when my children ask me something. I follow that up by saying, "We can look it up." The process of learning is very, very important to pass along to your children. By the way, they don't teach that in school anymore. Most schools are places where certified teachers simply open a textbook and run through drills without explaining the process of learning. As adults, your children will find themselves in situations where they have to switch career paths. How flexible they will be depends on how you have taught them to embrace learning, change and the learning process itself.

4. Continue training about your family's religion.

The instruction along those lines should have started as soon as the child could sit with you for reading and meals. Your religious organization will have materials appropriate for different ages. The Internet provides all sorts of printables as well. Even if it's just a coloring page you seek, that's a great way to add a craftivity at the end of a Bible (or religious) story.

You don't have to have a theology degree to share your faith with your child. I have found that my children ask me to tell them some of my experiences with God over and over again. They enjoy hearing how mommy was lead by God to different countries and through different (sometimes painful) experiences.

It does not take long, either. About 10-15 minutes a day is all you need to sing a couple of songs, tell them or read them a story, then let them work on a quick craft or a coloring page which drives the point home. And you're done.

If you don't talk to your child about God, somebody will. And it just might be the wrong person. A devotional is one of those daily habits which you should establish in your children early in infancy and continue as long as they are under your roof.

Like brushing teeth or practicing an instrument, it must be done daily.

5. Inspire your child to love spending time in nature, God's creation.

Love of nature comes from contact with nature. That's why I would recommend that you spend at least two hours outside, daily. No matter what the weather, children must spend time outside. It is essential for their physical, intellectual, and spiritual development.

In Sweden, they have a saying: "There is no such thing as bad weather. Only bad clothing." Swedish families will grill outside while the wind is howling and the rain is pouring. They have rain jackets and rain boots and hold an umbrella over the grill.

Have you heard of forest kindergartens? Rain or shine, students in a forest kindergarten spend time in nature. Their parents send appropriate clothing for the weather and these children make their own toys from twigs and leaves. Their teachers have certain lessons prepared, of course, and they do lots of singing and recitation, too. But it is all outside, in the forest (or their local park). And research studies have shown that forest kindergarten graduates go into first grade and perform very well academically.[5]

Fresh air and sunshine work wonders for the body. Exploring nature sets the foundation for studying science later on. Experiencing 3D objects now will help them theorize in upper grades. By the way, grasping theoretical concepts does not come easily to a child younger than 8, so don't expect that from your kindergarten student.[6]

Your children will find what to do outside instinctively. And they will observe leaves, birds, insects and animals without a lesson plan. I am not advocating forest kindergartens, but I am bringing it up to remind all of us that nature can be experienced no matter what the weather is like.

On my blog, www.HomeschoolWays.com, I write a series called *Wonderful Wednesday* about our adventures in nature. You might get some inspiration from there, as well.

6. Help your child learn to ride a bicycle.

Research documented by Frank Belgau in his book, A *Life in Balance*, has shown that the brain gets organized as we organize our physical movements in running, walking straight, and keeping our balance. I know parents who will not even teach a child how to read until that child can ride a bicycle without training wheels.

Personally, I believe that 5-10 minutes of phonics a day with a five-year-old will not hurt him, even though he does not ride a bike yet. But, I also believe kindergarten-age children must spend a lot of time outside running, playing in the sand box, hiking, learning to swim, tossing and kicking a ball and chasing butterflies or whatever else lives in their backyard and local park.

Of course, if you suspect a learning difference in your child, or if there is a family history of dyslexia, you will want to wait until your child can ride a bicycle without training wheels first. Then, you can tackle reading, writing, and arithmetic.

7. Introduce your kindergarten student to the 3 Rs.

Reading, 'Riting and 'Rithmetic are the foundation blocks upon which all learning lies. Don't fudge here. Don't rush ahead. Your child must be able to read phonetically, form beautiful letters by hand and know his math facts before he can go to the next level of using these tools for abstract learning.

But, again, the key word here is "introduce." Don't overwhelm yourself or your child with too much instruction during the kindergarten year.

8. Have your child start the study of a musical instrument.

Look for a teacher who jives with your child and your family's approach to education. A teacher that can accommodate you on a special day of the week might be necessary, as was the case for me (see Chapter 2).

Competitive need not be one of the ways to describe the atmosphere around your child's instrument learning. Children must be challenged, yes, but not stressed out.

Music study has so many benefits. Research shows that studying a musical instrument, especially piano, produces smarter kids.[7]

On the other hand, establishing a routine of daily practice, regardless of how motivated the child feels, will be the foundation of a great work ethic later in life. At least, that's what Aristotle seemed to think in this quote: "Good habits formed at youth make all the difference."

9. Teach your child healthy eating habits.

By the end of kindergarten, my son would pray that God would help him drink more water between meals, eat healthy and skip snacks. It's because I emphasized those healthy habits in our day-to-day interaction. By age five, your child should not need to snack between meals anymore.[8] Instead, give him water to drink – six cups of water every day is what a five-year-old needs. Replacing snacks with water keeps the body hydrated. It makes for a healthy appetite by meal time. It also keeps weight under control by providing oral pleasure with zero calories. Most American children are overweight these days, have you noticed?

Eating five daily servings of fruits and vegetables, washing hands after using the bathroom and before a meal, flushing the toilet, dressing in clothes appropriate to the weather and the activity pursued – these are all examples of habits which are best established now. For a funny take on the whole experience, read *All I Really Need to Know I Learned in Kindergarten* by Robert Fulghum. For me, this book reinforced the thought that my children did not need to attend school to learn important life skills.

10. Show your child how fun it is to be helpful.

The Moore Formula (MooreFoundation.com) in education has three components: work, study, and service. In this paradigm, academic study should take up as much time as work and service combined. Why? Because children learn so much more by doing than by studying.

A chore chart is a must. Explain to your child what his chores are for each day. Show your child how to do his chores at first. Then, supervise him doing it. Finally, you can let him do it on his own and only inspect the results.

It will take time in the beginning. Depending on the task, this three-step process might take a few days or a few weeks. It will feel like a chore for you to teach him how to do his chores.

I would encourage you to persevere. It is time well spent right now. As your child matures and learns to wipe a table, sweep a floor and put toys away, you will have an easier life in the upper grades.

CHAPTER 4:

10 WAYS TO KEEP

MOMMY SANE

"The grossness of motherhood strips all pretense of fashion and style.
We wear breast milk stained shirts and jeans with booger streaks at toddler
nose level, right around the knee." – Rachel Pieh Jones

1. Start a blog, not necessarily about homeschooling.

OK, so this may be a way to go insane really fast, too. It depends on how you approach it. If (1) writing comes easy to you and (2) blogging is more like journaling, i.e. working through your issues, then do it. If you want to blog in a professional way and start a content-marketing business, do it only if you are a very organized, detailed and motivated person. Blogging will give you something your own away from the children. It will put you in touch with other bloggers – a source of like-minded friends. It will even give you a way to get free resources for your website – in exchange for your honest review. Do it for long enough and, who knows, a book might come out of it. Again, if writing has always been your Achilles' heel, then move on over to #2 below and forget I even mentioned blogging.

2. Read non-homeschooling books.

Immersing yourself in worlds that are completely opposite of yours will give you a much-needed break from your daily struggles. The idea is to forget the tension and what caused it in the first place. You might even want to join a Book Club. Check with your local library. Most Book Clubs meet once a month for one hour. Even if you read for 20 minutes at night before going to bed, you should be able to get at least half way through any book by Club meeting time. Surely, hubby can handle the kids while you go mingle with other readers for one hour a month.

3. Read homeschooling books and blogs.

Let me clarify something here. I know a lot of homeschooling moms who blog. I am one of them. We don't do it to brag or to intimidate. We do it to inspire and help. We often show our own weaknesses, shortcomings, and the lessons we learned from a bad homeschooling day. If you feel intimidated by the homeschooling blogosphere, then steer clear. But, if you allow us to help you here and there, without comparing yourself to us, then I think you will discover that we are normal human beings, with baskets of laundry waiting to be folded and healthy meals waiting to be cooked. And we are willing to share our experience.

4. Attend at least one homeschooling convention a year.

There is nothing like walking the halls of a convention center and being surrounded by fellow homeschoolers. At my first convention, I was in tears of joy. I was a brand new homeschooler and felt like hugging everybody. I wanted to walk up to every person there and ask, "You, too? You mean, all these people here feel the same urgency, the same calling that I do?"

At my second convention, it was the same thing. I did not use to be somebody who cried easily, but homeschooling and my children have done a trick on me. The seminars will give you answers or more questions to ponder. Great food for thought. Some will encourage you and enlighten you. Others will make you laugh, relax, and realize it's OK to make mistakes.

Then, there are the products. How would you like to see, touch, feel (and even smell) those books you have only seen online so far? And what about the special pricing during the conventions? Do whatever you have to do to attend one convention per year.

5. Hang out with other homeschooling moms.

My local homeschooling group offers a Parent Support Night once a month. We get together, eat a potluck dinner and talk. I have missed it once or twice because I was tired. Staying in and going to bed early made more sense. But, every time I went, I had fun. I fellowshipped with other homeschooling moms, learned from them, shared with them, and exchanged tricks of the trade. There's nothing like it.

6. Enforce daily quiet time.

If you only have two children, like me, it might be hard to separate them for two hours. So separate yourself from them – if they are old enough. Go into your room and close the door. Make sure that you communicate with them about what they can and cannot do during quiet time.

Once you are in your oasis, do whatever you need to do to relax. Use this time for your creative outlet – crafting, knitting, cooking, blogging, whatever. Sometimes folding laundry and getting it out of the way is the most relaxing thing to me. Other times, I nap. Most days, I write.

7. Exercise and drink eight glasses of water daily.

Before my children wake up, I take a walk through our neighborhood. I chose a route that takes me about 30 minutes to walk at a brisk pace.

I bring my cell phone for safety and practical reasons. Walking while checking for any possible email emergencies saves me time because I know if I need to re-adjust my day when I get home.

Most of all, exercise helps me sleep better. I know plenty of women who cannot sleep and it's because of hormones. Well, exercise regulates hormones. Plus, it keeps you fit.

Drink eight glasses of water daily, between meals. If you cannot stand the taste of water, you can learn to appreciate it over time. Here's how to divide and conquer: two glasses before breakfast, while you do your devotions and morning exercise; two glasses before lunch, which you can start drinking about two hours after breakfast; three glasses between lunch and supper; one glass about one hour after supper.

8. Stay organized and keep a clean home.

See Chapter 9 for organizational tips, especially 10 forms which will make you feel on top of this homeschooling lifestyle.

Personally, I have days when I can't start homeschooling until we clear the clutter. My rule is to spend 10 minutes in the evening picking up our school room, which happens to be our living room/play room/dining room area. We don't always get to it though.

Things happen and we get off schedule. Next thing I know, it's too late in the day to clean. I give the kids a quick bath and supper. We read to them before putting them to bed. The day is over, but we wake up to a messy living room.

Who can think in a messy room? Not me. So we spend those 10 minutes in the morning. It really does not take longer than that if you do it every day. Granted, situations happen. After the children turned our living room into a circus (literally) and invited us to come enjoy the show, I knew we would spend more than 10 minutes undoing their play. But that does not happen very often.

9. Take a day or a week off from homeschooling.

You are the teacher. What if you did not plan a day off this particular week? When tension rises or your energy level is low, take advantage of your freedom as a homeschool teacher and declare a sabbatical. Let your child play all day while you relax.

Do what you feel like doing, whether it is reading, chatting with friends, gardening, catching up on chores, cooking a new recipe from scratch or doing nothing. Burnout is easier to prevent than to treat.

10. Take a trip.

It can be a virtual trip on Pinterest boards, or an actual trip without your husband and children. It does not have to be an overnight trip. Sometimes a two-hour shopping trip provides enough retail therapy to keep you going for another month or so.

Other times, a trip to your local art museum immerses you in other people's creative work. Thus, you can forget about your routines and problems.

CHAPTER 5:

10 FUNTASTIC

FIELD TRIPS

"School field trips had always been a welcome escape from routine, particularly when they'd involved aquariums or grown-ups dressed in colonial costumes." – Kristin Gore, "Sammy's House"

I'm more of a book lover, so I thought, surely, if I just read, read, read to my kids, they will learn, learn, learn. That is a true statement. However, children learn so much through hands-on activities. In fact, they need practical application of what they are reading about so they can retain their newly found knowledge.

Also, during a field trip, your children will acquire the kind of background knowledge that helps them frame and grasp the world around them. Field trips are like Velcro for their minds – more concepts have something to attach themselves to if the Velcro is there.

On a regular basis, I have had to put the books away and take my children on field trips. It started with a trip to our local fire station when they were three and one and it grew from there. As I went along, I realized any trip outside the home is a field trip.

Think about it. Learning happens everywhere you go. If you take a few minutes to share new vocabulary with them before the trip and reinforce it afterward as you ask them questions about the trip, you got yourself an unforgettable learning experience.

Here is a list of 10 funtastic field trips we have taken, which have enriched our children's knowledge of the world and have broadened their horizons in ways that books never could:

1. Zoo

From live animals to LEGO play areas, zoos offer just about anything to stimulate a child's mind these days. But the animals come first.

You have read to your child about different animals from books. Now the child can see just how big an elephant really is.

There may be bird shows and science classes especially offered for homeschoolers. There may be guided tours or interactive exhibits. A zoo is a great place to visit even on a cold or damp day, as long as they have an indoor play-and-learn area.

2. Aquarium

Where we live, we have an aquarium that offers science classes for homeschoolers. Also, they have lots of interactive exhibits where you can push buttons and pull levers to get different results as you learn about sea creatures.

They have a large room dedicated to one particular subject (past collections have included dinosaurs, slimy creatures, and sharks) and they change it every so often. They also have diving shows and feeding shows. There is no shortage of things to learn, see and do in an aquarium.

3. Children's Museum

Even if your local children's museum is a hole in the wall, you should give them a chance. Go once. You might be surprised by how much your children can learn from it.

Check if they have an annual membership so that you can return for special programs. Call ahead to see if they offer guided tours. Make sure you keep the museum ticket stubs for your records.

4. Petting Zoo

There are so many benefits in putting children and animals together. If you do not live on a farm, a petting zoo is the next best way to teach your children some zoology and what it might take to feed an animal every day. All the action happens outside, so your children will get fresh air and sunshine. Low-tech, 3D activities are vital to your child's brain development.

Most petting zoos will give you a little safety talk before they allow you to go inside. That's an opportunity for your children to listen to instructions from somebody outside your family and, of course, to learn safety tips.

Aside from its educational benefits, a petting zoo is great fun. My children really enjoy feeding the animals. They laugh and laugh when the emus stick their heads out through the fence to pick up grains from their cups.

Be sure to follow the safety rules of your petting zoo. Keep an eye on your children at all times. But, even if you do, please know that there will be tears. Your children might get licked by a horse (it happened to my daughter) or might be slightly bitten by a camel (it happened to my son). It's part of it.

5. Doctor's office

Most doctors will understand if you bring your children along. In fact, some of them (and their staff) relish seeing little people. It breaks up the routine of their adult world day.

Your children learn so much from being in a doctor's office, whether they are the patients or not. My children have seen me get allergy shots and they even saw a small surgical procedure on my arm (to remove a suspect mole).

A few years ago, I wore braces. I still go to my orthodontist on a regular basis for follow-up appointments. That's a bit of a preparation for when they start wearing their braces. It also teaches them they will have to be responsible and wear their retainer at night or whenever recommended, after the braces come off.

I take my children to a pediatric dentist, but they also come to my dental appointments and see me get dental care. They hear the discussions I have with dental professionals and realize brushing teeth and flossing have good consequences. Not brushing and flossing have bad consequences.

Good habits are easier to establish if we understand the reasons for them and the consequences for not having them.

You know what they say: knowledge is power. Give your children medical facts and they will be more likely to develop internal motivation for a healthy lifestyle. Taking them to the doctor helps them learn these facts in a relaxed way.

6. Grocery store

A few years ago, a friend of mine was trying to decide whether to put her child in a private school or homeschool him. When she looked more into the private school of her choice, she learned that one of the field trips was to go to the grocery store. There, the children got to name fruits and vegetables, write down prices for ingredients necessary for a particular recipe, and watch somebody pay and transport their groceries to the car.

Hmm... Do you really have to pay $4,000 a year to an establishment so they can take your child to the grocery store? Of course, you pay for 179 other days of education and they may be well worth the money. But my point is that even supposedly superior schools will not do something for your child that you cannot do yourself as you homeschool him.

If you play a game of vegetable (or fruit or money) Bingo before or after the trip, you got yourself a fun and engaging school day. You can make the cards yourself or download them from one of the generous bloggers out there who share their resources with the world for free.

7. Library

It's a fact. Children who get taken to the library on a regular basis get better scores on their tests, as documented in the first half of *The Read-Aloud Handbook* by Jim Trelease. Besides learning the process of borrowing books from a library, your children can also learn social skills.

Story time is a chance to mingle with other children and to learn that there is a time to listen and a time to talk. Greeting a librarian, responding to a compliment, and doing small talk are important life skills. I know because I come from a culture where small talk is not practiced or taught. I have had to learn it as an adult in order to come across more friendly here in the USA.

Some librarians might be a bit hostile to you or your children because they have a prejudice against homeschoolers (or, maybe, just because they are having a bad hair day). That's a chance to show graciousness and a forgiving spirit. You can discuss it all afterward with your children.

Don't limit yourself to visiting just one library, if possible. We live near three different libraries within a 30-mile radius. I have a card for each one. As my children get old enough, I will get them cards for each one, as well.

One library is the closest and most convenient for us to attend Story Time. Another has great funding from Dolly Parton herself, so their book collection is impressive. The third one boasts an $11,000,000 state-of-the-art building with great meeting rooms and programs. We are blessed.

8. State or National Parks

We happen to live nearby the most visited National Park in the United States, so it's easy to hike regularly, attend Junior Ranger

Programs in the summer, and be in the know about other events throughout the year.

Even if we didn't, we would probably make the effort of taking a trip to a National Park at least once a year. Check with their Visitor Center. They have maps and day hike brochures for free or a nominal fee. Hiking is great exercise and allows for time spent together as a family. It promotes having a conversation. Hiking is also a wonderful way to connect with nature.

State parks also offer birding, hiking, and nature study. Visit their website or call ahead to check schedule and availability of camping sites, picnic areas, and hiking trails. Sometimes the weather or a mud slide disrupts their regular schedule.

9. Camping

It's no secret, children love camping. And, parents, camping does not have to mean roughing it. But, if it did, it would make you so much more grateful and aware of the blessings you maybe take for granted (like running water and electricity). After two nights in a tent, you will be thankful for your bed, too.

So do your homework, invest in some gear that might make camping more comfortable (like a pad to slip under your sleeping bag, a propane stove etc.) and make some memories with your children. They will have fun and you might discover some simple pleasures yourself.

Learning how to start a fire, set up and take down a tent, bike safely, protect oneself from sunlight and insects, recognize poison ivy and share a camping area with others are valuable life skills.

10. Concert Hall

Concerts don't have to be expensive. In fact, some are free. You just have to look around for opportunities.

We live an hour away from a city which boasts a symphony, an opera, and several theaters. They even have a youth symphony orchestra – five of them, actually, on different levels based on age and skill.

The youth symphony orchestra concerts are free. What a great way to inspire your children to persevere with their instrument learning. What a great way to teach music appreciation.

I started taking my children to these free youth symphony concerts when my youngest was two. It was not easy, but, somehow, God gave me the strength to do it. We learned to sit near an exit so we don't disturb too many people when it's time to leave.

CHAPTER 6:

10 INSPIRING

KINDERGARTEN CURRICULA

"Instead of a national curriculum for education, what is really needed is an individual curriculum for every child." – Charles Handy

Every curriculum in a vendor hall stems out of a philosophy of education. You must inquire what that philosophy is before you buy.

In my book, *101 Tips for Preschool At Home*, I outline and describe the 10 main homeschooling philosophies or methodologies: classical, Charlotte Mason, unit studies, Montessori, delayed academics etc.

No doubt about it, your curriculum choice can make or break your homeschool. Some people don't even have a kindergarten curriculum though. It depends on the law where they live and on their – there's that concept again – educational philosophy.

In an online forum, this lady scoffed at the idea of a kindergarten curriculum and said, "We played a lot. And we went to the zoo." You can tell she has an unschooling philosophy or a better-late-than-early approach by her answer. That's all fine for her, but some people feel the need for a curriculum. Yet others must show for four hours of learning a day where they live. It's the law of the land. My guiding light as I pick curriculum is *The Well Trained Mind* by Susan Wise Bauer. I also follow Charlotte Mason principles and the Moore Formula. If you really needed to put a label on my homeschooling style, it would be eclectic, because I combine three methodologies. So here are some inspiring kindergarten curricula we have used and enjoyed. These have worked for us and I will explain why. Even if you disagree from the start with these choices, reading about them will help you discern what curriculum will feel more comfortable to your teaching style or your child's learning style:

1. *The Ordinary Parent's Guide to Teaching Reading*

For teaching reading, I believe in a solid phonics textbook, devoid of pictures. The mind does not need to make a connection between a picture and a sounded out word, then to a bunch of letters. I have found *The Ordinary Parent's Guide to Teaching Reading* to be very easy to use. I cannot recommend this curriculum more, especially if you are scared of teaching phonics. The things you have to say are even scripted out for you, should you need some help interacting with your child. The activities and games are fun. Preparation time is minimal. To me, that is a must in any curriculum. That's why I pay for it. I don't want to do a lot of other work (scanning, printing, laminating, getting lots of manipulatives together etc.) besides actually teaching the curriculum.

2. Logic of English – *Rhythm of Handwriting*

I believe in teaching cursive first and only. There is a whole debate on cursive vs. manuscript. I have reached my conclusion based on personal experience and research. I was taught cursive first and only and I know it works. From the research I have done on both sides of the argument, I have seen the advantages of cursive first from a theoretical point of view, as well.[9] So here I am, I can do no other.

If you are in the other camp, which advocates manuscript first, fear not. Logic of English also has a manuscript curriculum, although they, too, advocate you start with cursive first. As to printing needed for filling out forms later on in life, children can learn to print by themselves. My four-year-old just started copying letters in her thank you notes to grandparents, because she wanted to keep up with big brother. Not all kids are that motivated that early though.

If you wanted to give your child formal practice in printing upper case letters, that is fine, of course. However, please keep in mind that writing requires fine motor skills. There is no reason to start teaching writing in preschool, just as there is no reason for baby to read. Again, if your child shows an interest, show them the strokes and let them do some pre-printing practice. But don't make it a long lesson. I wrote 1,000+ words about our experience with Logic of English Cursive, so I invite you to visit my blog post about it: http://homeschoolways.com/rhythm-of-handwriting-review.

Suffice it to say that we loved it and my son could write a three-letter word in cursive after two weeks of instruction. He was six and five months old.

3. *Right Start Mathematics*

This Montessori-inspired math curriculum is rather different from the textbook-workbook method you might be used to. It uses an abacus, which is a tool that has helped budding mathematicians for millennia.

Math games provide the needed practice in Right Start Mathematics – not pen-and-paper drills. It took me a while to get away from feeling that my child was not getting enough practice. You, too, might have to adjust a bit to a new paradigm.

The placement test on the Right Start Mathematics website showed us we needed to get Level B and that's where we are today. We did not finish Level B in kindergarten. We continued with it through first grade. When it moved a bit too fast for him (or for me), we stopped and played the card games. Or, I supplemented with Math Mammoth.

4. LEGO Education – *Simple Machines*

If you have a LEGO fan in your home, you will want to invest in one of these LEGO Education set. Go ahead and splurge. Get the binder. The CD-ROM is nice to have, but navigating between teacher's notes, student's worksheets and building instructions is very awkward. The binder is worth the extra money.

Both my children have used this curriculum and have learned science principles, vocabulary, and the scientific method through it. Besides, it is a lot of pure LEGO fun.

Just like with any LEGO project, you will have to exercise a lot of oversight in order for the bricks, plates and other elements to be returned to their proper box and trays.

5. *My Bible Friends*

Stories will make your Bible class and family devotional times interesting. Your children will look forward to Bible class. Written in the 1950s, these five volumes and the two accompanying CDs contain beautiful English and accurate biblical details.

Listen to the CDs in the car or pop them in your children's CD player at night after they go to bed. Use them during their afternoon quiet time. Use them as your child follows the words on the book for extra reading practice.

6. Petra Lingua – Foreign Languages

In Kindergarten, children are still highly wired for foreign language acquisition. Take advantage of this window of time and introduce them to the sights and sounds of a foreign language. Small children like animals and your kindergartner will love Wuffy, the mascot at Petra Lingua. We are using this curriculum for French.

Full disclosure: they are one of the sponsors of my blog, but I chose them first. I liked the lesson plans. This is serious language learning – repetition and drills abound – but they are veiled in an atmosphere of play and songs. One can purchase the offline kit, with DVDs, CDs and workbooks, which comes with a hand puppet Wuffy, or an online subscription.

There are 21 lessons which build on each other. For instance, the lesson on school supplies is followed by the lesson on colors. During the lesson on colors, the school supply vocabulary is revisited as we see a "yellow book bag" or a "blue crayon." The same goes for numbers and other concepts.

If you don't speak French at all (or any other language offered by Petra Lingua), you can still use it for your child. Native speakers pronounce all the words and there is time allotted for repeating back what you hear. Who knows? You might even learn some French in the process.

7. KinderBach.com – piano lessons for different levels

Another gentle curriculum, perfect for a Kindergarten student, is KinderBach.com. The teacher is wonderful in her presentations – not too silly, but not too serious, either. There are coloring sheets, a series of cute animals and a boy who act as reminders of what the notes are. For instance, Dodi is a donkey and his house is between the two black keys. If you don't have time to drive to piano lessons, KinderBach.com is a great alternative. For a thorough review of this curriculum, please visit my blog, http://homeschoolways.com/kinderbach-com-review/.

8. Lapbooks from HomeschoolShare.com

First off, these are free. Before you spend money on other sites which produce lapbooks, you ought to take a look at HomeschoolShare.com, under the Lapbooking category on the main menu. There is a master list of all free lapbooks and then there are separate lists organized by level and topic. I really like the ones based on books. You can read the books first to your kindergartner, then work on the lapbooks together.

A word of caution here: lapbooks are great if your child enjoys cutting and pasting. If you have a boy, like I do, you might discover that he gets tired of it easily. So I break it down into small chunks and I help him out a bit.

The important thing is for him to have fun and go over some of the new vocabulary and concepts from the book you just read together.

9. *Life of Fred* – Math

I know people who use *Life of Fred* as their main curriculum in kindergarten because they believe in a very gentle introduction to academics for a child that age. *Life of Fred* is not our main curriculum. It is a supplement. We really, really like it. We tailor it to our student's needs, too.

The author strongly recommends that your child work all the exercises at the end of each chapter with pen and paper. We tried that and, after a while, my son got tired of it. He wanted me to read the book and not do the exercises.

I worked with him on his attitude first, then we reached a compromise. We did the exercises orally. You see, at the time, my son was really bored with kindergarten math – we actually switched math curriculum mid-semester, as I shared above. So, having that background, I allowed us to veer off the recommended path.

All this to say, make the curriculum your own. If your child shows enthusiasm about the exercises, go right ahead. If your child balks at them, read the story and move on, or try doing some orally.

You know your child better than anybody else. It's your decision and your homeschool. Don't be afraid to adapt your curriculum to your child's needs.

Notice I wrote "needs" and not "wants." I know my child does not need more busy work. He knows the concepts already. We practice math enough during our main math lesson, using *Right Smart Mathematics*.

10. Science4us.com

Dr. Jay Wile, Apologia founder and curriculum author, recommends hands-on science experiments and simple notebooking experiences after nature walks through grades K-6. He himself wrote great science curriculum for those ages. However, he will also tell you that if you need to skip anything on a tough homeschooling day during the early elementary years, science should be it.

Having said that, small children like science experiments and exposing them to science vocabulary and concepts in a relaxed way will not hurt them.

That's what Science4us.com could be for your homeschool. It's there if you need an hour of peace and quiet while your child is being educated about scientific concepts.

We used it and my children learned a lot. One of the lessons that really stuck was recycling. All of the sudden, they wanted to keep every single box and bag we threw away. They would take it and decorate it and play with it for many weeks.

I have a full review of Science4us.com on my blog: http://homeschoolways.com/science4us-com-review/. For your information, Science4us.com assumes evolution as fact, but it only brings up evolutionary concepts in one or two lessons.

CHAPTER 7:

10 HELPFUL HINTS FOR

READ-ALOUD SUCCESS

*"It is a rock, approximately two feet across. It is roughly
textured, gray in color, but a portion of it is flat and smooth as grass.
From this surface comes a glowing light that is quite beautiful
and pleasing to look at." – Chris Van Allsburg, "The Wretched Stone"*

One of the best ways you can spend your time in kindergarten is to read aloud to your children. Start with *The Wretched Stone* by Chris Van Allsburg – an allegory of what TV watching does to people.

Several celebrities have come out to speak against TV and its detrimental effects on children. These are people who make a living by being on TV or in movies, mind you. But they know it is trash.

Here are 10 tips to make reading aloud a successful experience:

1. Turn off the TV.

We all know that TV watching reduces creativity and robs us of precious time. I don't like to give myself as an example, but some people wonder how I can write a biweekly newspaper column, publish several blog posts a week, run a LEGO Club and a French Play Group, teach two classes at my church, and write books while homeschooling my two children. The answer is simple: I do not watch TV.

I don't have time to sit and watch what other creative people are doing. I am doing. My children benefit from it because they have a living proof in the home that evenings can be spent reading, making music or engaging in other creative projects (like writing). Evenings do not necessarily mean TV watching.

My husband, who reluctantly agreed to homeschool, read aloud to the kids, and turn off the kids' videos, has seen the results in our children. He is a convert to the policy of turning off electronics and encouraging books.

Our son started kindergarten reading on a third grade level. He entered first grade reading on a fifth grade level. I am not advocating early reading skills. I believe every child reads when they are ready for it, given the proper instruction. I am just sharing that, in our experience, turning off the TV increased literacy.

2. Understand the difference between reading level and listening level.

A six-year-old can read a couple hundred words, but can understand several thousand words. So don't insult his intelligence by keeping him on a picture book diet. He needs to start on classics and chapter books.

Transitioning need not be a difficult process. You just start where you are, with the books that you think your child might be interested in, and you read. That's it.

3. Read *The Read-Aloud Handbook* by Jim Trelease.

This may actually be the greatest book on the subject, with research showing you why and how to read aloud to your children. Want the skinny? You can save a lot of money on college tuition if you train your children to enjoy books by reading aloud to them.

So for the nights when you just feel too tired to read to the kids, psych yourself up with the mantra, "Scholarship, scholarship, academic scholarship!" I jest, of course, but the fact remains that your children will be on track for a high SAT score and a possible National Merit Scholarship if you spend 30 minutes daily reading to them. The second half of the book contains the golden lists of books that should be read aloud, organized by categories. This is a reference book. You want it in paper format, so that you can refer to it over and over, make notes in the margins, and share with a newbie homeschooling mom in your group.

4. When you read aloud, slow down.

The biggest mistake I made in the beginning was to read to my children too fast. My mom overheard me read to my children a few years ago and asked if there was a fire. I slowed down.

Then, we bought some CDs corresponding with a 5-volume Bible story series called *My Bible Friends*. I heard professional narrators read the story and learned some more. And I slowed down some more. I also added voices and some sound effects. Not too much. Just enough to make it interesting.

If somebody knocks on the door, I reach for the closest wooden object so I can knock. If an animal is mentioned, I make that animal's sound (unless it is a rabbit or an ant). If somebody yawns, I yawn. Next thing I know, my kids yawn, too. It's fun.

5. Explain new words as you go by.

You can read a lot to a child, but, if you don't explain new words, you will not improve their vocabulary. Some children will ask what "regimen" means. Many will not. If you think your child may not know a certain word, provide a synonym or a short explanation and move on. Don't make it into a lesson or a lecture. But do provide a quick meaning for new words. My children usually let me know if they already knew that word.

6. Always read one challenging book.

By challenging I don't mean boring. For instance, I found that my children do not like non-fiction books that simply describe a river or a mountain or an animal. But if I give them non-fiction books in a story format, I have their full attention.

When they were five and three, I started reading picture books with more words on the page: a paragraph instead of a sentence or two paragraphs per page even. It created a bit of tension, but we worked through it. Challenging them now and then is good. It takes away the impression that they might be experts, which is easy for a small child to believe. It's a bit of a balance: you want to keep them engaged through a strong story line, while bringing more vocabulary. Giving definitions quickly helps.

As your children grow, you will be able to read through nonfiction books. It's a matter of timing and watching for signs of readiness. The most important thing is to have fun and to relax. Your children will let you know if you push them too hard and if you bore them to tears. Trust your instincts, continue doing your research and things will work out.

7. Separate kids only if more than two years apart.

If your children can sit together and enjoy the same material, even though their comprehension levels may be different, by all means keep them together. The above is simply a rule of thumb.

I have talked to moms of four children who manage to keep their children together for many school activities, including reading aloud. Sometimes the older children take turns reading. But, most of the time, the fascination is with mommy's voice and, so, the task belongs to mom.

8. Transition to longer picture books when your oldest child is almost five.

Longer picture books do not have to have more pages. They just have to have more words on each page. Your child will gradually focus longer and pay more attention to detailed descriptions. Over time, he will be able to grasp several characters and their involvement in the plot. If the younger child protests or gets restless, you have two options: either you separate them for this longer book, or you ignore the protests and put up with the restlessness.

For me, at least, my youngest always wanted to sit in my lap. Her restlessness affected my ability to hold the book and see the words.

So I got firm with her in a nice tone and said, "You either sit here and don't move or go play while I finish this book for your brother."

Well, she has always wanted to do what big brother does. It worked. She focused, stayed put and did not bother me again. At least, not for that session. Over a period of three months, she did better and better and now she sits through chapter books like *Heidi* and *Lassie* and she is four.

9. Transition to chapter books when your oldest is six.

Chapter books come in many forms. Some have shorter chapters and pictures. Others have longer chapters and no pictures at all. You should start with the shorter ones – that's common sense. If they come with pictures, even better. Slowly, you should be able to get into longer chapters.

If the story grips your child, length will not be an issue. So give your book a chance – read the first couple of chapters. If your child is not engaged, ditch the book altogether. There's no need to struggle through a difficult book.

10. Don't ask for a book report after every book read.

Beware of busy work. Reading aloud should be fun. If the child knows that after every book read he is to sit down and write the name of the author, the title of the book, the copyright date, the publisher, the number of pages, plus draw a scene or write about the plot, he will dread every new book you bring.

It's best to do this once in a blue moon. Try every five books or once a week.

CHAPTER 8:

10 MUST-BUILD LAPBOOKS

"The world in general doesn't know what to make of originality; it is startled out of its comfortable habits of thought, and its first reaction is one of anger." – W. Somerset Maugham

Lapbooks are inexpensive portfolios or manila folders filled with mini-books, flaps, pockets and images – an interactive, creative way for your child to display their knowledge. Because they usually fit in the lap of a child, they are like books in a lap – hence the name.

Lapbooks should be an integral part of learning in your homeschool and especially so in the early grades. Children are not abstract thinkers at this stage. Instead, they need concrete experiences to hang words and concepts upon.

Keep a basket or box only for lapbooks. By the end of the year, showing off ten manila folders and all their colorful pockets and art work should impress homeschool-skeptical grandparents.

But that's not why we lapbook. We lapbook because it's a great way to learn while developing fine motor skills from handling the scissors; because we learn new words as we build vocabulary lists; because we remember what we have done with our hands; and because young children need concrete, 3D experiences as they acquire new concepts.

So you have 36 weeks of kindergarten and 10 must-build lapbooks. Once a month, you could print out one lapbook and get your child busy. Plan to spend several sessions on a lapbook.

For an organized approach, pair the themes with the seasons, holidays and your other curricula ahead of time. You will need manila folders, paper, card stock and a printer. Sometimes a brass fastener or two, a stapler, and some scotch tape. Glue is a must.

The internet is replete with lapbook ideas and you can see videos on how to make your own lapbooks. We use HomeschoolShare.com (free lapbooks organized by grade) and HandsOfAChild.com (one free lapbook every month, which may or may not be on your child's grade level, as well as sales throughout the year).

We glean ideas from Jimmie's amazing Squidoo lenses on lapbooking and from LapbookLessons.com. On the download page of each individual lapbook at HomeschoolShare.com, you will find an Amazon widget showing you book titles that go along the theme of that particular lapbook. Write them down and get them from your library if you don't necessarily want to own them.

Here are my 10 must-build lapbooks for kindergarten:

1. The Ten Commandments

If your family's spiritual heritage draws from Judeo-Christian roots, I don't have to explain why this lapbook is important. If you are not a Christian or a Jewish family, your child should familiarize himself with The Ten Commandments. They are the basis upon which Western Civilization has been built.

My friend Rhonda, who blogs at PreparationEducation.com, has put together a lapbook which lists the 10 commandments. Just click over to her site and choose Lapbooks in her list of Categories on the left. The templates are at the bottom of the page. You will find some other great lapbooks in this category on her blog, too.

2. Spring

HandsOfAChild.com has a lovely garden and spring theme lapbook called "In the Garden: Flowers and Insects," which you can supplement with other ideas from around the web.

3. Summer

Just because it is summer vacation, learning doesn't stop. In fact, this is when learning is most fun, because it is not mandatory. So feel free to put together a summer themed lapbook or get working on Summer Olympics from HomeschoolShare.com.

4. Fall

Five Little Pumpkins, Turkey Time, Thanksgiving, Harvest Time – all these and more can be found on HandsOfAChild.com. The sky is the limit with the pockets and artwork you could create for your own take on a fall lapbook, of course.

5. Winter

As you work on Winter Sports or Christmas Cheer from HandsOfAChild.com, or a lapbook from HomeschoolShare.com based on the book "A Snowy Day," you will surely get rid of cabin fever during long winter months.

6. Officer Buckle and Gloria

First of all, read the book several times. It is hilarious AND it emphasizes safety. Then, build the lapbook with your small children (from HomeschoolShare.com). It contains very important safety tips, which may save a life – although one always hopes one never has to face such extreme situations. Also, it teaches your child his full name, address, when to dial 9-1-1 and other concepts. Safety really should be our number one priority.

7. The Human Body

The Prekindergarten and Kindergarten section at HomeschoolShare.com (they call it Level Two) has a great lapbook on the subject. This should get your children interested in taking care of their bodies while teaching them anatomy and physiology.

8. Healthy Foods

The books and corresponding lapbook under the name Grocery Store on HomeschoolShare.com will give you a great start. The themes covered are: grocery store, shapes, colors, money, coupons, food groups, and healthy eating. As with any lapbook, your children will improve their fine motor skills, sorting, tracing, and cutting abilities.

9. My Family

HandsOfAChild.com offers a graphics pack called All About Me and, also, a project pack called Discovering My Family Tree.

10. Phonics

Short and Long Vowels from homeschoolshare.com. Very cute and useful – like all lapbooks, really. Children must engage all their senses to learn at this stage. Phonics is as abstract a subject as they come.

A word of caution about the picture cards. Personally, I don't like phonics books with pictures. The brain does not need to make the connection from picture to letter to sound. It's more complicated a route. Instead, the brain must be taught to go from letter to sound.

If you object strongly to pictures in phonics exercises, you can eliminate the cards with pictures altogether. I used this lapbook with my children when one was in kindergarten and the other one in preschool. As such, for the sake of the preschooler, we used the picture cards. But I did not make this lapbook THE way to learn phonics.

CHAPTER 9:

10 FORMS TO KEEP

YOU ORGANIZED

"And the Lord answered me: 'Write the vision; make it plain on tablets, so he may run who reads it.'" — *Habbakuk 2:2*

Whatever your vision is for your homeschool, you should seriously consider putting it on paper. The Bible promises that if the vision is plainly written out and you read it, you will run with it. Research has proven that most people who write down their goals actually go on to accomplish them.

Some moms are planners. Others are good record keepers. Common sense tells me that you need both to a certain degree in order to stay organized. Both are needed to show your child's work throughout the year, should anybody ask.

In addition to the school forms below, you might find it useful to have forms for a monthly menu, a grocery list, and a chore chart.

On my blog, HomeschoolWays.com, you can download a free ebook with several organizational forms. The ebook is called *21 Days to Jumpstart Your Homeschool*. It is a devotional and a workbook that will help you get into new habits and a new routine.

I was in my first year of homeschooling when I wrote it, so I knew exactly the feelings of a confused newbie, who needed to put order in the chaos of keeping house while doing academics.

Here are the 10 forms that will help you divide your life into manageable bits and conquer them one by one:

1. Master Calendar

You don't need to spend money on fancy planners. The Internet will help you out with all sorts of free printables. A simple blank yearly calendar, with individual pages for each month, can get you started.

A good plan today is better than a perfect plan tomorrow. Don't feel that you need elaborate to-do lists and cute designs to stay organized. Personally, I use Google Calendar. It fits easily in my purse – because it's on my cell phone. I can access it on my laptop as I discover new events I might want to attend with my children.

But I plan my curriculum and my blog on paper, with pencil. See point 10 below.

2. Daily Schedule

Say "schedule," but think "routine." Life will get you off the daily schedule you wrote down. Don't let that frustrate you. Think about it. If you went to work outside the home, it would be the same thing.

You would have certain projects to work on, but emergencies would pop up.

So don't fret if it does not work out, but have a schedule, a routine. It will help you know where you are once the interruptions are over. Thus, you can get back on track.

3. Curriculum List

You may live in a country or state where the law requires that you present a list of curricula used. Or, you may have to operate under an umbrella school which asks for a list of curricula.

Even if you don't, I think you should have a simple form which lists the subjects in one column and the textbooks used in another. If nothing else, it will help you know if certain curricula work or not. If you have other children coming behind your kindergartner, this curriculum list will become invaluable.

4. Reading Log

I did not keep reading logs for the first six years of my children's lives. I regretted it. You don't have to notate copyright information or the illustrator's name. The title and the author are all you need. Keeping a running reading log is best done on the computer – it's easier to search and alphabetize your list that way.

If you read a lot of books from the library, they may be able to produce a list of the books you check out. My local library does it monthly.

Yet another option is to keep the little receipts the library prints for you every time you check out books. I have a sheet protector in my child's reading binder and I slip each one of these receipts in as we get a new one. Sure, some titles may appear on two receipts, but, at least, I have some record of what my child has read.

Bonus: the library receipt also provides the date – a wonderful souvenir for a future scrapbook.

5. Book Report

As soon as your child is ready to draw a scene from a book, you should encourage him to produce a book report. Like anything, take this advice with a grain of salt and in the context of a thriving homeschool – minimize busy work.

If it becomes a chore and it discourages your child, don't require a book report after every single book read. If your child does not enjoy putting pen on paper, then he will start dreading read-aloud times because he knows a book report is looming on the horizon.

So make it fun and, if a book really catches his imagination, ask him to draw a scene from it. Otherwise, you can ask him questions about the book orally and let him narrate back to you his impressions of the story.

6. Field Trip Log

Apparently, college admission officers go back into your child's records. Way back. Further back than ninth grade. Wouldn't it be great if you could produce a pocket of museum tickets and Legoland stubs from your child's kindergarten year? All it takes is a paper or plastic pocket inside your child's kindergarten binder, labeled field trips, and a simple field trip log showing the date, the location, and the main concept learned.

Documentation is extremely important. Somebody once said to me, "If it's not in writing, it does not exist." Should you ever run into problems with the truancy police in your school district, you have something to show for your efforts. This is especially the case because you may want to be out and about with your kids during school hours. Some people, filled with good intentions, will report you when they see you around town during school hours.

7. Service Opportunity Log

This is another great log to have – for your own benefit, not just for the officials. You know those days when you feel like you have not done enough, when you have misgivings about this whole homeschooling adventure, when you question whether you are doing enough for your children?

That's when you should pull out the service log and the field trip log and everything else you keep records on and say to yourself, "Look at all these educational experiences my child is having. Of course I am doing a great job. The Lord has called me to this and has given me the energy to accomplish all this. I can do it. I am doing it. I have done it."

My son played the violin in a nursing home when he was in kindergarten. He was new at violin playing, so you can imagine how squeaky he sounded. But the patients loved it and he loved it, too. That's a service opportunity. We made cookies for our neighbors at Christmas time. So many good things came out of that simple gesture. I told the kids, "Kindness comes back."

8. House Rules

Unacceptable behaviors and their consequences should be listed and presented to your child at the beginning of the school year and on a regular basis. Or, better yet, as soon as you finish reading this paragraph. Any institution has rules to abide by. Your children should know your house rules and the consequences for breaking the rules ahead of time. Don't come up with too many rules though. If you need more than two sides of a letter-size paper, you probably have too many rules. But, and this is the most important part, you should enforce them. Consistently, you should send the message to your child that your communication is always truthful. That he can trust your word. That you love him enough to give him consequences, so that he can learn his lesson.

9. Attendance Record

Some of us live in places where we need to school for 180 days in a calendar year. There are plenty of calendars online which you can print for free. All you have to do is put a check mark in each box which corresponds to a day you schooled. By the way, record keeping does not overwhelm. It really does not take longer than five minutes to record your day in the evening.

10. Lesson Planning

These are not your individual lesson plans. Lesson Planning refers to having a semester-long calendar with the book names and chapter numbers you cover each school day. This will help you understand what you need to do in order to finish by a certain day in May or June. This will give you so much peace of mind on days when you just can't seem to pull yourself together.

Even if you miss a day here or there, you will know that you can still make up for it.

By the way, once the 180 days of school are over, you can continue to teach your children and avoid the summer slide, as they call it in educational circles.

So you have even less reasons to worry about not keeping up with your lesson planner. But that does not mean you should not plan. You can relax because you know you have a plan. It is a flexible plan, but you have one and know when you must press forward and when you can afford to pull back a little.

I like The Old Schoolhouse *Hey Mama Planner* for curriculum – it comes in a digital as well as paper form. I have used both, but right now I am in a pen-and-paper stage.

CHAPTER 10:

10 NO-PREP ACTIVITIES

WHICH COUNT AS SCHOOL

"We can be tired, weary and emotionally distraught, but after spending time alone with God, we find that He injects into our bodies energy, power and strength." – Charles Stanley

Raise your hand if you ever have low-energy days. My hand is raised, just to let you know. I am no super-woman. I am no Energizer bunny. After an exciting field trip or after several long days in the homeschooling trenches, exhaustion catches up with me. Other times, I just feel blah and need a break.

By all means, when you feel like taking a break, take one. I recommend that as one of the 10 sanity savers under Chapter 4. But what if you cannot afford to take another break? What if you feel too guilty to take a break for your own sake? What if you are on the homestretch before the end of the semester or even the school year?

Here are 10 activities you do not need any energy for. They are educational, fun, and, best of all, you can jump right in, with hardly any preparation:

1. Reading to your children

For us, reading aloud is fun. We have a solid library of quality children's books in several languages and we read, read, read. Morning, evening, afternoon, we read. Sometimes we ask our son to read – he was an early reader and, lately, he enjoys showing off his reading skills. It also gives our mouths a break, too.

It's not hard to send them to the book shelves to bring you what they want. This will insure they are fully engaged with the material and learning will happen.

Please see Chapter 7 for hints on how to read aloud to your children.

2. Story time at the library

Is it that day of the week again? The day when your local library is holding their story time? Get the kids in the car and go. They are likely to do a craft and some singing, too, in addition to being read to. And all this time, you can sit back and relax in the back of the room.

Of course, you can take mental notes of their behavior and knowledge they might show if prompted. Make sure you record this activity in your homeschooling report for the day.

3. Hiking or nature walks

If the weather is nice and you have no desire to open a book, chances are your children will not want to do that, either. Get their bikes, helmets, and pads and hit the trails. If you feel you must, bring along their nature journal or a sketch book, a pair of binoculars, a camera, and a small picnic (PBJs and apples work just fine).

Learning will happen as you observe nature and practice biking skills. Record it under science as nature study or under P.E. as exercise. Regardless, it's school time and you did not have to do much to prepare.

4. Building LEGO Education models

No energy? No problem. Just pull out a LEGO Education set and let your child build. You can worry about the lesson plans later.

If your child happens to be a LEGO fanatic, you will not hear any protests out of him. You can take two minutes to congratulate him and go over new vocabulary with him in a casual way. "I like how you added that winch to the truck," for instance. If you feel he needs the stimulation, you can suggest a small experiment, which he can do on his own. "Have you tried testing how fast your sail boat will go if you put a fan behind it?"

Then, he is back to his self-directed study, while you can return to your rest or whatever you were doing. You just gave yourself another 20 minutes of uninterrupted time.

5. Educational apps

Full disclosure – I am not a big fan of educational apps and video "learning" games. However, I recognize that, at times, a relative full of good intentions may have given your child a gizmo that's supposed to teach him academic skills.

If you allow your child 30 minutes of a learning game once in a blue moon, I don't think it will destroy his good intellectual habit of reading and actively engaging in the learning process.

Meanwhile, you get some rest, weary homeschool mama. You deserve it. Tomorrow is another day.

6. Science4us.com or similar programs

My children learned so much from Science4us.com. Months after they finished the program, they kept talking about some of the lessons. Among other things, they learned to re-cycle. Since then, they have made toys for themselves from pretty much any box, small or big, which I would otherwise throw away.

Again, I am not for high-tech educational experiences. But, on your low-energy days, allow your children to teach themselves as they navigate an online course. It's a win-win.

7. Talking books (in another language, too)

Reading is fundamental. No reading, no decent future. One of the things you can invest in are things similar to V-Tech's Bugsby collection of books. They have a stylus which, when they touch to certain areas of the page, engages a sensor. A voice reads to them the entire page or only certain words.

It's not a substitute for a solid phonics program, but it's something that they can learn from while you rest.

If it's in another language, it's even better.

8. Instrument practice

You can hear a child practicing from another room, can't you? You don't even have to be right there. But a kindergarten student needs guidance, so it's recommended that you sit with him as he practices. How much effort does it take, really, to supervise a few minutes of instrument practice? You can do it. Then, you can record it as music and there, another learning activity just took place in your homeschool, on a low-energy day even.

9. Speaking to your children in your mother tongue, if it is different than the language of instruction

I realize this does not apply to everybody. It's only for those of us who have another language and have been using it with our children since birth. My children are bilingual. I address them in Romanian 80% of the time. They answer me in English 95% of the time. But I count Romanian as their mother tongue or a foreign language, if you will, in our homeschool. Because it is hard to quantify it, I record one hour daily. And I truly need no prep work for this.

10. Listening to audio books in the car

On a low energy day, when you absolutely must go somewhere or run errands, get the kids in the car and turn on an audio book. They will be quiet, which will give you some peace so you can gather your thoughts. Learning is happening, so you are doing school. We call it car schooling and we use it all the time. No prep work necessary, no high-level of energy needed.

I use regular CDs in my car's CD player, or MP3 CDs which I play through a portable DVD player and a cassette adapter ($10 at Walmart). Another great way to play audio books is on my Kindle Fire with the cassette adapter.

By the way, you can get great children's classics for the Kindle for free or less than $3 and then it is another nominal fee for the audio version. That's how you get around $20 audio books or those Audible monthly fees.

CHAPTER 11:

TIP 101

*"The only person who is educated is the one who
has learned how to learn and change." – Carl Rogers*

The hardest thing you will have to deal with during your kindergarten year is motivating your student to come to the table. Even if you only do half an hour of phonics, tracing letters and counting with bears, even if the rest of your school is made up of fun projects your child loves, you still will have a hard time getting your five-year-old to come to the table. That's it. That's Tip #101.

Being aware of the greatest struggle you will encounter will help you more than you realize. I have talked to several people who were very, very discouraged during their first year of homeschooling because they had this uphill battle against the will of their five-year-old child. Every single one of them questioned the decision to homeschool because of it. "If I have to struggle like this just to bring this child to the table, then homeschooling is too hard. I don't think I have what it takes to homeschool," one mom said to me.

Awareness is the first step because knowledge is power. Stay with me. Keep reading. There are solutions ahead.

The second step toward conquering this problem is learning what motivates your child. You have no doubt heard the quote, attributed to several people, that "Education is the kindling of a fire, not the filling of a bucket." How do you motivate a child to learn? How do you kindle his fire?

Observe your child. What does your kindergartner like to do? How does he spend his free time? What kind of imaginative play does he engage in of his own free will? That's your clue.

Diana Waring tells the story of a homeschooling mom who could not get her son to learn the alphabet. He loved his baseball cards though, so his mother saw her opportunity there. She said to him one day, "How would you like to learn a way to organize your cards so you can find a certain one quickly? It's called alphabetizing." She got his attention. He learned the alphabet in half an hour. The next day, he taught his younger brother the alphabet. That's the power of motivation.

The third step you must take is to relax. Your child is only in kindergarten. There may be some burnout going on. Perhaps, some immaturity. There may be some parenting issues that need to be addressed between you two. Does the child always disobey when you ask him to do something? Then it's not homeschooling or burnout or immaturity. It's parenting. If you are relaxed and do not take his refusal personally, you can focus and find out why your child refuses.

Last but not least, consider the context of the refusal. Did your family just go through a sad time – like losing a pet? Did you just get back from an exciting trip? Did you just say goodbye to family members after a family reunion? Is your child coming down with something? Through it all, as you continue to pray for wisdom, have confidence in yourself and in God. You will figure out how to motivate your child.

By the way, you will also learn that what worked last week may not work today. Up on your toes you go! Many times, when working with intelligent kids, it's hard to figure them out. Also, please remember that we all have bad days. Children are no different.

Trust your instincts and do what works. Don't push the pen-and-paper activities for awhile. Read to your kindergartner, let him play outside, involve him in the kitchen and around the house in chores, and try again next week. Time works wonders.

There's no need to get discouraged because your kindergartner will not come to the table. You have plenty of time to teach him academic skills. For now, focus on life skills and character. The rest will come when he is ready.

In 2 Peter 1:5, we are admonished, "... add to your faith virtue; and to virtue knowledge." You cannot add to faith unless you already have faith. So faith comes first. Then, virtue. Virtue is another name for character. Finally comes knowledge.

Please do not think that I am not for strong academics. I am all for challenging intellectual pursuits. But the Bible is clear that first and foremost we must teach our children faith and character. Knowledge comes in the third place.

So spend the kindergarten year teaching your child about the God you believe in, help him develop good habits, and, if he is ready, spend some time at the table doing school.

May the Lord bless your efforts as you embark on your official homeschooling journey.

ABOUT THE AUTHOR

Adriana Zoder is a polyglot, author, newspaper columnist, and homeschooling mom of two. Born in Romania, Adriana Zoder also lived in Sweden before moving to the United States and becoming an American citizen.

The first volume of the *How to Homeschool* series, *101 Tips for Preschool at Home*, is available in paperback and Kindle formats on Amazon.

Adriana's blog, HomeschoolWays.com, received an award from Homeschool Blog Awards Post and ranked in the Top 10 Best Homeschooling Blogs at voiceBoks.com.

You can connect with Adriana through her blog, HomeschoolWays.com, and on Facebook, Twitter, Pinterest, Google+ and LinkedIn.

REVIEW REQUEST

If you enjoyed this book and found it useful, I would be very grateful if you posted a positive review.

Please go to the review section on the book's Amazon page.

Click on "Create your own review" and share your experience with others. I read all reviews in order to learn from my readers.

Thank you in advance,

Adriana

NOTES

1. Pamela Druckermann, *Bringing up Bébé*, p. 79-80.

2. Ann Voskamp, aholyexperience.com, *Joyful Parenting Manifesto* (PDF).

3. From Dr. Jay Wile's talk, *Homeschooling: the Environment for Genius*, Appalachian Home Educators Conference, Pigeon Forge, June 27, 2014.

4. Raymond and Dorothy Moore, *Moore Formula Manual*, p. 87.

5. http://en.wikipedia.org/wiki/Forest_kindergarten

6. http://en.wikipedia.org/wiki/Piaget's_theory_of_cognitive_development

7. http://www.telegraph.co.uk/science/science-news/6447588/Playing-a-musical-instrument-makes-you-brainier.html

8. http://www.ucheepines.org/snacks-and-eating-between-meals/

9. https://www.logicofenglish.com/blog/44-handwriting/122-why-teach-cursive-first

LIT
FRC

43384178R00054

Made in the USA
Charleston, SC
26 June 2015